MONSTER MOVERS

by Richard Gunn

GARETH**STEVENS**
GS
PUBLISHING
A Member of the WRC Media Family of Companies

Please visit our Web site at: www.garethstevens.com
For a free color catalog describing Gareth Stevens Publishing's
list of high-quality books and multimedia programs,
call 1-800-542-2595 (USA) or 1-800-387-3178 (Canada).
Gareth Stevens Publishing's fax: (414) 332-3567.

Library of Congress Cataloging-in-Publication Data

Gunn, Richard.
  Monster movers / Richard Gunn.
    p. cm. — (Cool wheels)
  Includes bibliographical references and index.
  ISBN-10: 0-8368-6827-7 – ISBN-13: 978-0-8368-6827-2 (lib. bdg.)
  1. Earthmoving machinery—Juvenile literature. I. Title. II. Series
TA725.G86   2006
621.8'65—dc22   2006042295

This North American edition first published in 2007 by
Gareth Stevens Publishing
A Member of the WRC Media Family of Companies
330 West Olive Street, Suite 100
Milwaukee, WI 53212 USA

© 2006 Amber Books Ltd.

Produced by Amber Books Ltd., Bradley's Close,
74–77 White Lion Street, London N1 9PF, U.K.

Project Editor: Michael Spilling
Design: SOL
Picture Research: Terry Forshaw and Kate Green

Gareth Stevens editorial direction: Valerie J. Weber
Gareth Stevens editor: Jim Mezzanotte
Gareth Stevens art direction: Tammy West
Gareth Stevens cover design: Charlie Dahl
Gareth Stevens production: Jessica Morris

Picture credits: QA Photos Ltd: 5; Caterpillar: 7, 17, 25, 29; Komatsu: 9; Bucyrus International Inc.: 11;
P&H Mining Equipment: 13; Liebherr: 15; Le Tourneau, Inc: 21; Terex Mining: 27.

Artwork credits: Richard Burgess (© Amber Books): 4; Marshall Cavendish: 6, 10; Komatsu: 8; Mark Franklin
(© Amber Books): 12, 16, 20, 22, 23, 24, 28; Liebherr: 14; Brookes & Vernons: 18; Terex Mining: 26.

We would also like to thank the following manufacturers who sent us reference material for artwork images:
P&H Mining Equipment; Caterpillar; Le Tourneau, Inc; Gomaco Corporation.

Printed in the United States of America

1 2 3 4 5 6 7 8 9 10 09 08 07 06

CONTENTS

ROBBINS TUNNEL-BORING MACHINE

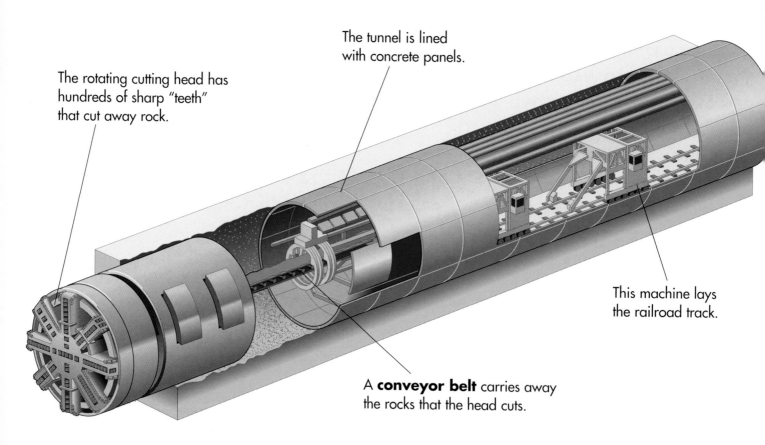

The rotating cutting head has hundreds of sharp "teeth" that cut away rock.

The tunnel is lined with concrete panels.

This machine lays the railroad track.

A **conveyor belt** carries away the rocks that the head cuts.

Left: The large cutting head that bites into the rock is at the front of this tunnel boring machine.

A tunnel boring machine, or TBM, makes large tunnels.

ROBINS TBM

First Year Made: 1977
Size: 39 feet (12 meters) wide by 600 feet (183 m) long
Amount Bored: 100 tons per hour
Power: 3,084 **horsepower**

It can bore, or dig, through mountains. It can even bore beneath water. Tunnels are needed for roads and railroads.

Gigantic Worm
A TBM has a large rotating head. When this head moves forward, it cuts through rock. The pieces of rock are sent back through the machine on a conveyor belt. The TBM moves forward slowly, leaving behind a finished tunnel. It works like a giant mechanical worm!

DID YOU KNOW?

Trains and cars travel between England and France through the Channel Tunnel. It lies beneath the English Channel, a stretch of sea that separates the two countries. Robbins TBMs dug the Channel Tunnel, which was completed in 1990.

CATERPILLAR D10 BULLDOZER

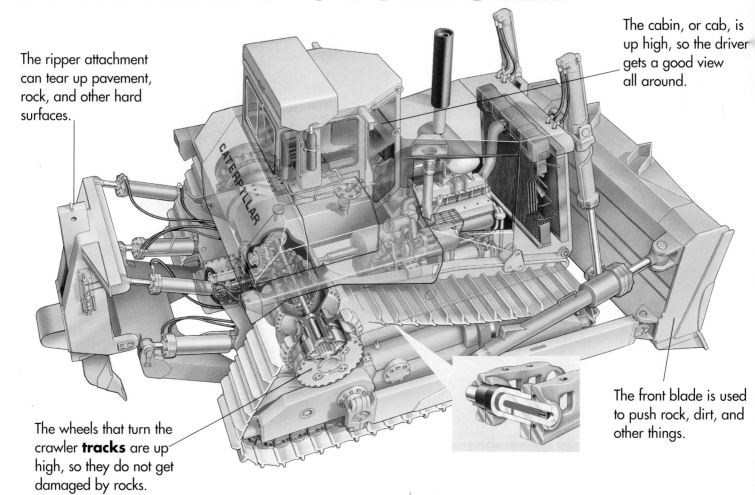

The ripper attachment can tear up pavement, rock, and other hard surfaces.

The cabin, or cab, is up high, so the driver gets a good view all around.

The front blade is used to push rock, dirt, and other things.

The wheels that turn the crawler **tracks** are up high, so they do not get damaged by rocks.

Caterpillar began making the D10 in 1977. It soon became one of the most popular **bulldozers** in the world.

High Drive

When it first appeared, the D10 was the most powerful tracked "dozer" around.

It has crawler tracks instead of wheels. The tracks are metal belts.

CATERPILLAR D10

First Year Made: 1977
Size: 30 feet (9 m) long by 12 feet (4 m) wide
Load Amount: 29 cubic yards (22 cubic meters)
Power: 520 horsepower

Wheels turn, or drive, these tracks. On most machines, these drive wheels are near the ground. The D10's drive wheels are up high, so they have less chance of getting damaged from rocks or the ground.

The D10 has a tall, wide blade. It can push huge loads. The D10 is powerful and reliable. This dozer can handle the toughest jobs.

DID YOU KNOW?

Engineers who made the D10 first built a small model using parts from an old lawnmower. When they tested it, they found it was strong enough to pull a Jeep!

KOMATSU D375A-2 BULLDOZER

The blade could push a medium-sized car.

A thick roof and side bars protect the driver if the bulldozer rolls over.

Hydraulic arms move the ripper, too.

Hydraulic arms move the blade. Oil gets pushed through the arms. The oil forces out long, shiny tubes, called **pistons**. They move the blade.

The **transmission** sends power to the drive wheels that turn the tracks.

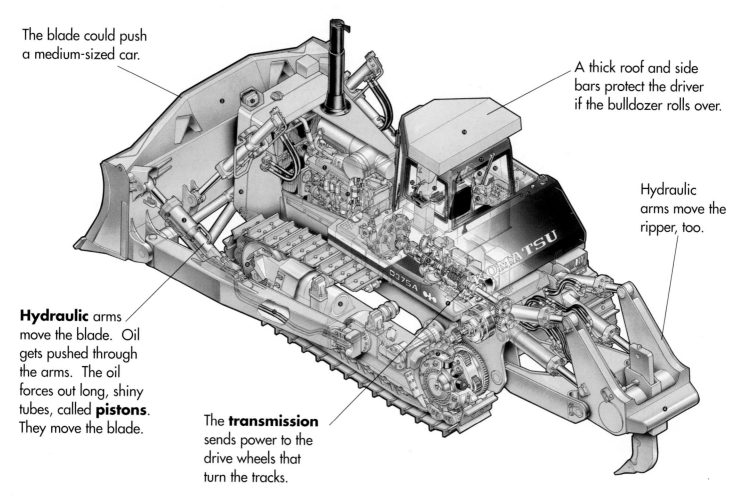

The Komatsu D375A-2 is a big machine, but it is small compared to some bulldozers. With its small size and low height, it can reach places and do jobs that bigger machines cannot. It can get into narrow spaces, such as tunnels and trenches, and it can fit on narrow roads. With its crawler tracks,

Left: Even on loose, slippery ground, the bulldozer can keep working because of its crawler tracks.

KOMATSU D375A-2

First Year Made: 1987
Size: 34 feet (10 m) long by 15 feet (5 m) wide
Load Amount: 29 cubic yards (22 cubic m)
Power: 525 horsepower

it does not need a lot of room to turn around.

Slow but Powerful
This bulldozer is not fast. Its top speed is 7 miles (11 kilometers) per hour going forward and 10 miles (16 km) per hour going backward. Riding a bicycle, you are likely to beat it! But it can move earth, rocks, and even buildings. It does not need to be fast to do its job.

DID YOU KNOW?

The word "bulldozer" comes from the old-fashioned term "bull-dose" — a really hard shot, or dose, of something. If you hit something hard, you give it a bull-dose!

BUCYRUS-ERIE 1550 WALKING DRAGLINE

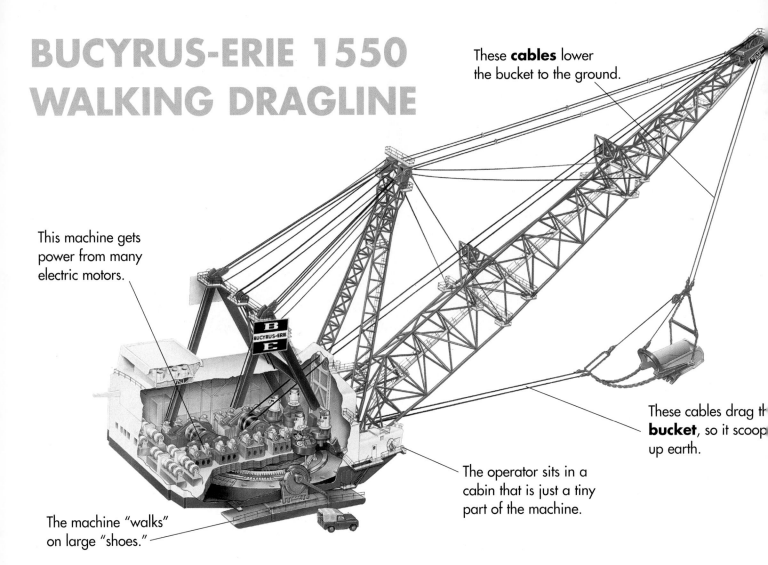

These **cables** lower the bucket to the ground.

This machine gets power from many electric motors.

These cables drag the **bucket**, so it scoops up earth.

The operator sits in a cabin that is just a tiny part of the machine.

The machine "walks" on large "shoes."

Walking **draglines** are some of the biggest machines ever to work on land. They can be as tall as office buildings. These **excavators**, or diggers, usually work at **mines**. They are so large, they have to travel to a mine in pieces.

At the mine, many workers put the dragline together. It usually works at just one mine.

Left: A Bacyrus-Erie 4250-W dragline moves earth at the Muskingham mine in Ohio. Called "Big Muskie," it is the largest walking dragline ever built.

BUCYRUS-ERIE 1550

First Year Made: 1967
Size: 487 (148 m) long by 151 feet (46 m) wide by 186 feet (57 m) tall
Bucket Load: 100 tons
Power: 6,250 horsepower

Excavators often get named after the workers who use them — the 1550 was called "Big George"!

A "Walking" Machine

A dragline has no tracks. Instead, it rests on large "shoes." As these shoes rock back and forth, the dragline "walks." The machine moves very slowly — it travels just 840 feet (256 m) per hour. You could easily outrun it!

DID YOU KNOW?

In England, a dragline similar to the 1550 once "walked" a distance of 13 miles (21 km) to a new work site. It needed nine months to complete its journey.

P&H 4100XPB ELECTRIC SHOVEL

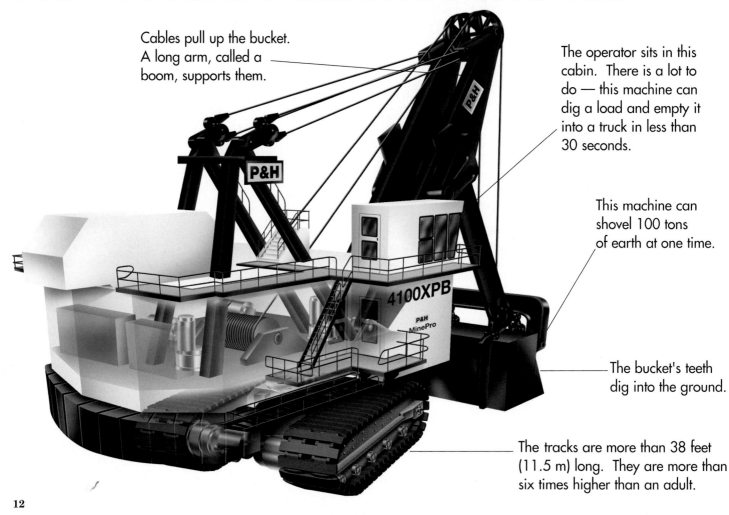

Cables pull up the bucket. A long arm, called a boom, supports them.

The operator sits in this cabin. There is a lot to do — this machine can dig a load and empty it into a truck in less than 30 seconds.

This machine can shovel 100 tons of earth at one time.

The bucket's teeth dig into the ground.

The tracks are more than 38 feet (11.5 m) long. They are more than six times higher than an adult.

An electric shovel digs upward with its bucket. It is different from a hydraulic excavator, which digs down into the earth. It is also different from a dragline, which drops and drags its bucket.

The 4100XPB is one of the best electric shovels in the world. The machine has computers onboard to help it work better.

Left: The cab is high off the ground, so the operator can see what is being loaded.

Electrical Power

This huge digger has powerful electric engines. They get electricity from a thick cable that unrolls behind the digger. The cable is like a giant extension cord!

This machine costs twelve million dollars. It will keep working for many years.

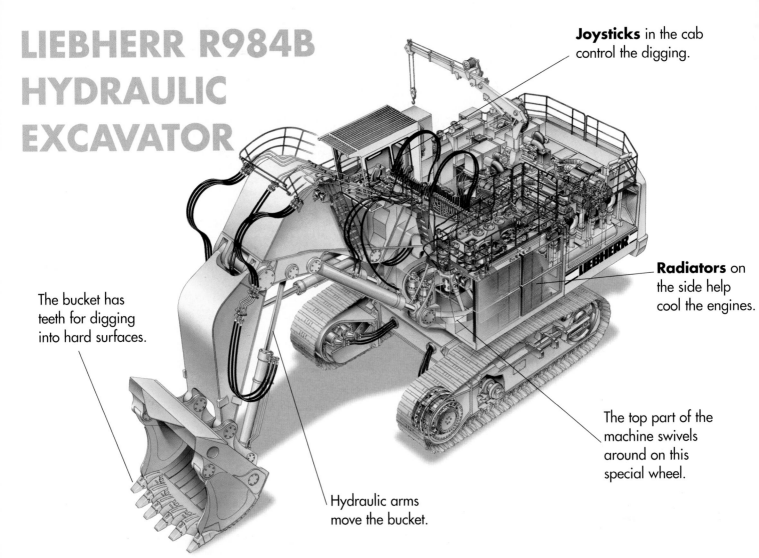

LIEBHERR R984B HYDRAULIC EXCAVATOR

Joysticks in the cab control the digging.

Radiators on the side help cool the engines.

The bucket has teeth for digging into hard surfaces.

The top part of the machine swivels around on this special wheel.

Hydraulic arms move the bucket.

Despite its great size, an excavator such as the Liebherr R984B can really get around. Its tracks allow it to travel on rough or soft ground without getting stuck. The bucket is on a hinged arm, so it can dig in hard-to-reach places. The machine can stay in one place while it digs, because its top part swivels around on its bottom part.

Left: This excavator is digging down into rock. Its tracks help it move on uneven ground.

LIEBHERR R984B

First Year Made: 1995
Size: 60 ft (18 m) long by 17 feet (5 m) wide
Bucket Load: 14 tons
Power: 510 horsepower

Dig and Demolish

This machine has powerful hydraulic arms. Its bucket has sharp teeth for digging into hard materials. It can even demolish buildings.

The excavator can dig down below the ground it is on, and it can also scoop out hillsides. It can swing around to load a waiting truck, so jobs can be finished quickly.

DID YOU KNOW?

Crawler tracks were invented in 1770. They work better than wheels on rough surfaces because they carry weight more evenly. They keep a machine from sinking into soft ground.

CATERPILLAR 163H GRADER

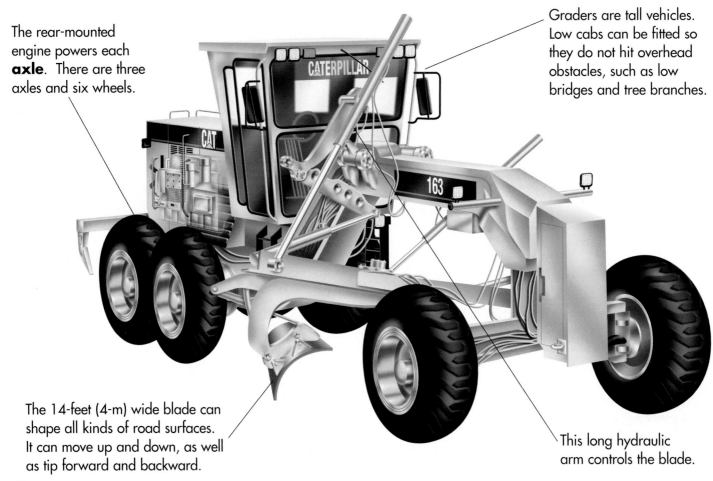

The rear-mounted engine powers each **axle**. There are three axles and six wheels.

Graders are tall vehicles. Low cabs can be fitted so they do not hit overhead obstacles, such as low bridges and tree branches.

The 14-feet (4-m) wide blade can shape all kinds of road surfaces. It can move up and down, as well as tip forward and backward.

This long hydraulic arm controls the blade.

This strange-looking vehicle is a motor grader. It is mostly used for building roads.

After a scraper has removed earth, the grader makes the ground level.

Six-Wheel Wonder

The cab and engine sit above the two back axles. The blade is mounted on a bar that connects to the front

CATERPILLAR 163H

First Year Made: 1994
Size: 33 feet (10 m) long by 8 feet (2 m) wide
Scraping Speed: 27 miles (43 km) per hour
Power: 257 horsepower

wheels. As the grader moves forward, loose rocks and dirt are moved aside by the blade, leaving a smooth surface behind. Concrete or **asphalt** can then be put

down to make a paved road. The weight of the engine is spread evenly over the four back wheels, so the 163H can keep a good grip on slippery surfaces.

DID YOU KNOW?

The top speed of the 163H is just 27 miles (43 km) per hour. It can reach almost the same speed going backward.

JCB 456B LOADER

A computer screen in the cab lets the driver know if there are any problems with the **loader**.

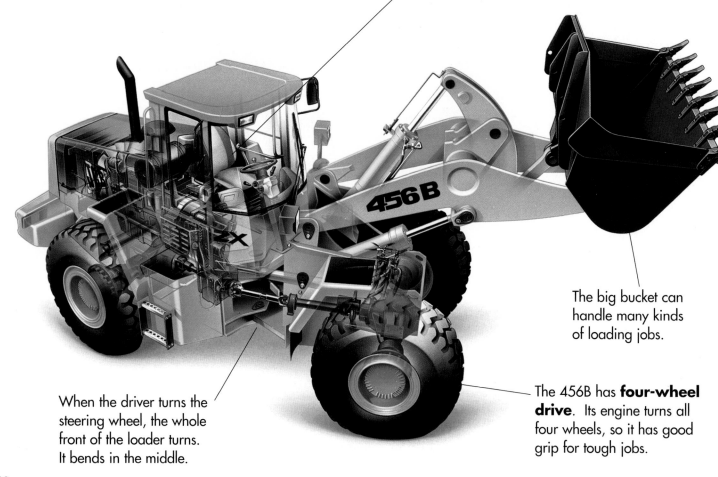

The big bucket can handle many kinds of loading jobs.

When the driver turns the steering wheel, the whole front of the loader turns. It bends in the middle.

The 456B has **four-wheel drive**. Its engine turns all four wheels, so it has good grip for tough jobs.

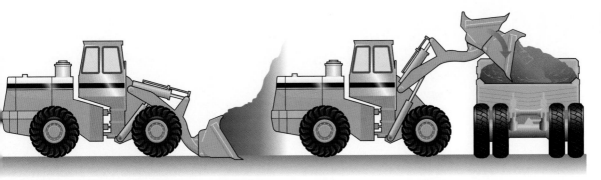

Left: The hydraulic arms of a loader let it scoop up earth and drop it into a large dump truck.

The loader is one of the most useful vehicles ever invented. Loaders are used on many kinds of jobs, from building highways to moving blocks of hay on farms.

Moving Loads

A loader can move material by holding it in its large front bucket. It can pick up rocks, dirt, and even trash. It can then drop its load into dump trucks.

JCB loaders are easy to spot, because they are always painted in a bright yellow color.

This loader has tires. Other loaders have tracks, but they are slow and can damage paved surfaces. Loaders with wheels are often used in towns and cities.

With its tall, wide tires, the JCB can travel on all kinds of roads and rough ground.

JCB 456B

First Year Made: 1998
Size: 28 feet (8.5 m) long by 9 feet (3 m) wide
Bucket Load: 7.5 tons
Power: 216 horsepower

DID YOU KNOW?

When working in cities or on roads, loaders often carry workers' tools in their buckets. The workers do not have to carry the tools themselves.

19

LE TOURNEAU L-2350 WHEEL LOADER

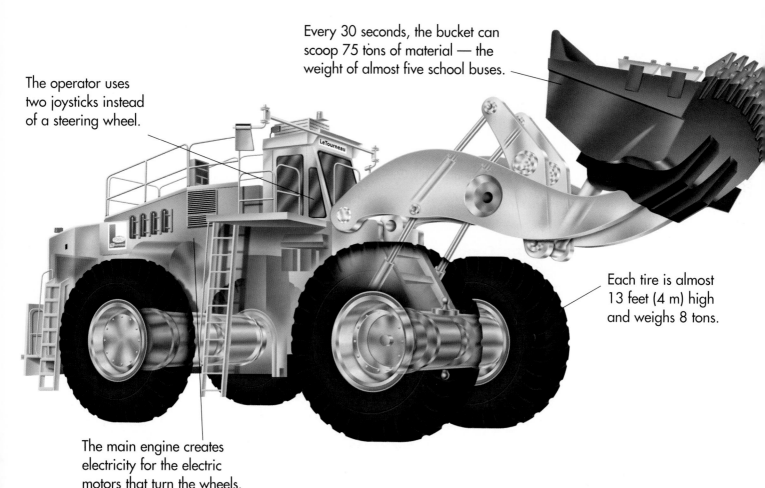

Every 30 seconds, the bucket can scoop 75 tons of material — the weight of almost five school buses.

The operator uses two joysticks instead of a steering wheel.

Each tire is almost 13 feet (4 m) high and weighs 8 tons.

The main engine creates electricity for the electric motors that turn the wheels.

Left: The L-2350 can fill the biggest dump truck with five loads in just two minutes!

Le Tourneau's L-2350 is the world's largest wheel loader. It works in mines. Ten trailers haul it in pieces from the factory to a mine, where it is put together. Once in action, the L-2350 works all day, every day, both shoveling and loading material into dump trucks.

A Thirsty Worker
Its big engine uses 54 gallons (205 liters) of fuel every hour. This amount is equal to about fifteen full gas tanks in a normal car!

LE TOURNEAU L-2350

First Year Made: 2000
Size: 66 feet (20 m) long by 22.5 feet (7 m) wide
Bucket Load: 75 tons
Power: 2,300 horsepower

DID YOU KNOW?

The Le Tourneau L-2350 uses the world's largest loader tires. They were designed just for it. Four workers take thirteen hours to make just one tire.

GOMACO GP4000 CONCRETE PAVER

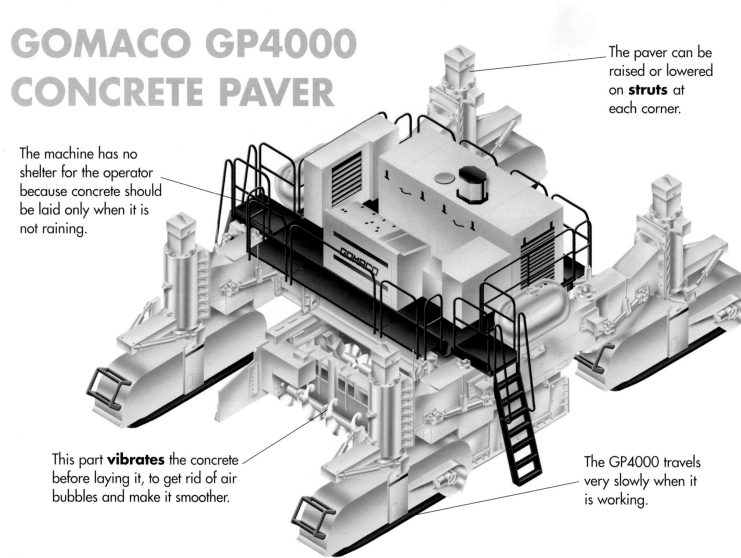

The paver can be raised or lowered on **struts** at each corner.

The machine has no shelter for the operator because concrete should be laid only when it is not raining.

This part **vibrates** the concrete before laying it, to get rid of air bubbles and make it smoother.

The GP4000 travels very slowly when it is working.

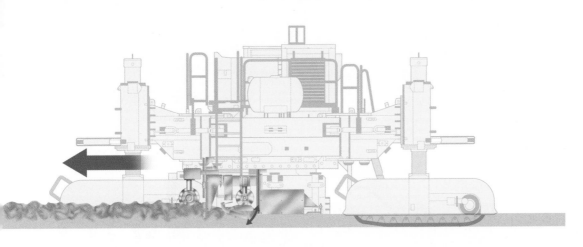

Left: The paver slowly creeps forward, laying and smoothing the concrete with its screed as it goes.

Pavers are very important for building roads and airport runways. These machines put down a layer of concrete and smooth the surface.

Pavement Maker

The machine works by first passing over the layer of crushed stones that form the bottom layer of the road. Concrete, which is carried inside the paver, is poured over the top using a **screed** — a large flat plate that is the same width as the road being paved.

Then, the paver moves forward, and a flat surface is left behind. This surface is smoothed before it fully dries, and the road is complete.

GOMACO GP4000

First Year Made: 1994
Size: 31 feet (9 m) long by 58 feet (18 m) wide
Paving Speed: 31 feet (9 m) per minute
Power: 450 horsepower

DID YOU KNOW?

Concrete pavers first appeared in the early 1900s in North America. During World War II (1939–1945), they were often used to make runways for military aircraft.

CATERPILLAR 657E SCRAPER

The **hopper** is like a large bowl. It can carry more than 100,000 pounds (47,170 kilograms) of material — the weight of three cars.

A hitch attaches the rear section to the front section.

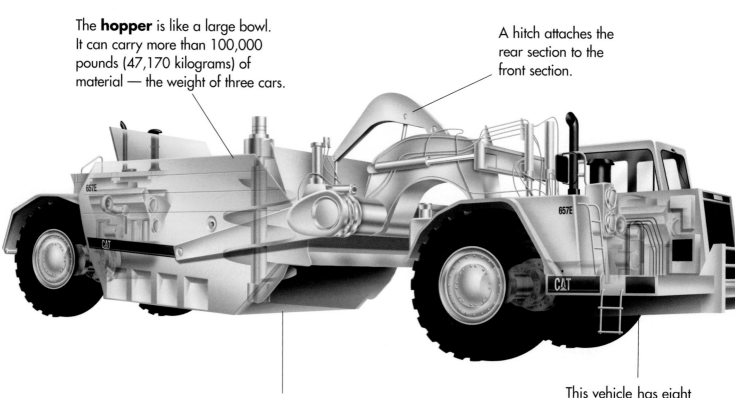

The blade can cut into the ground 20 inches (50 centimeters) deep.

This vehicle has eight forward **gears**, so it can travel at many different speeds while scraping.

Left: The hopper on this scraper has been lowered to the ground. As the machine moves forward, the hopper fills up with a load.

The Caterpillar 657E is a huge **scraper**. Its job is to make the ground level. This machine can scrape away hills and fill in low areas. The hopper at the back is lowered down so it scrapes along the ground, scooping up material as the vehicle travels along. When the hopper is full, it is raised and the scraper is driven to a place where the load can be emptied.

Double Effort

Big scrapers need a lot of power to scrape up large chunks of earth. The 657E has two large engines. Despite its power, the machine moves very slowly.

CATERPILLAR 657E

First Year Made: 1981
Size: 53 feet (16 m) long by 14 feet (4 m) wide
Top Travel Speed: 31 miles (50 km) per hour
Power: 1,350 horsepower

DID YOU KNOW?

For big, tough jobs, two scrapers may be hooked together. The two scrapers work as a team.

TEREX 4066 ADT TRUCK

The **diesel** engine sits far forward, ahead of the front wheels. Its weight helps balance the load in back.

Forty tons of material can be carried in the **bed**. It can tilt far back without the truck tipping over.

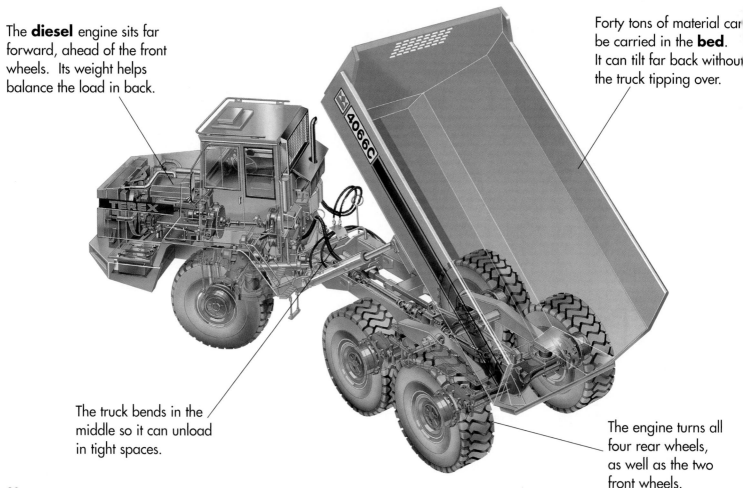

The truck bends in the middle so it can unload in tight spaces.

The engine turns all four rear wheels, as well as the two front wheels.

This truck is called the 4066 for two reasons. First, its bed can carry a 40-ton load. Second, its engine turns all six wheels, to help move the load.

You need to be up close to one of these trucks to appreciate how big they are. With its bed raised, a Terex 4066 has a height of 23 feet (7 m) — about four times taller than an adult.

Left: With its bending middle, tight corners are no problem for the Terex, even with a full load.

TEREX 4066 ADT

First Year Made: 1996
Size: 34 feet (10 m) long by 12 feet (4 m) wide
Load Amount: 40 tons
Power: 400 horsepower

Tight Turns

This Terex dump truck is used for off-road work only — for mining and for moving earth. When doing this work, it must be able to steer easily and move into difficult spaces, despite its huge size. For this reason, the truck bends in the middle to turn, and the front wheels always stay straight.

DID YOU KNOW?

In 1974, Terex built the largest dump truck of all time. It was called the Titan, and only one was built. When it stopped working in 1990, it was displayed in Canada, at the mine where it first worked.

CATERPILLAR 797B DUMP TRUCK

It takes only 25 seconds to raise the bed — even with a full load — and just 18 seconds to lower it.

The driver climbs these stairs to reach the cab.

The tires are more than twice the height of an adult. Each one weighs three times more than a typical car.

The Caterpillar 797B is the largest dump truck working in the world today. This monster mover is used for taking material from mines. It can carry a total load of 380 tons, which is 102 tons more than its own weight.

Power but Not Speed

Despite its very powerful engine, the 797B moves slowly. With a full load,

CATERPILLAR 797B

First Year Made: 2002
Size: 48 feet (15 m) long by 33 feet (10 m) wide
Load Amount: 380 tons
Power: 3,550 horsepower

it has a top speed of 42 miles (68 km) per hour on a flat road. Considering its big load, this speed is quite fast!

Its size means that it cannot change direction easily. The turning circle is the distance a vehicle needs to turn around in a complete circle. Most cars need about 35 feet (11 m). This truck needs 132 feet (40 m)!

DID YOU KNOW?

Some 797Bs have special engines so they can work high up in the Rocky Mountains, where the air is thinner.

GLOSSARY

asphalt — a material used to pave roads.

axle — the shaft that a wheel spins around.

bed — the part of a dump truck that carries loads.

bucket — the part of an excavator or loader that scoops up earth, rocks, and other materials.

bulldozers — vehicles that travel on tracks and have large blades in the front for pushing and scraping.

cables — metal ropes made of strands of wire.

conveyor belt — a wide belt that travels on rollers to carry things from one place to another.

diesel — the name for a kind of engine and the special fuel it uses. Most diesel engines are very reliable.

draglines — giant excavators that dig with a bucket that drops down from a long arm. Cables, or lines, drag the bucket to dig rock and earth.

engineers — people who make or design engines and other machinery.

excavators — large machines that dig.

four-wheel drive — a system that sends the engine's power to all four wheels.

gears — small, toothed wheels. The many gears in a transmission allow a vehicle to travel at different speeds.

hopper — a large container that is used for carrying material. It usually empties on the bottom.

horsepower — the amount of power an engine makes, based on how much work one horse can do.

hydraulic — referring using a liquid to move something, such as a bucket on an excavator.

joysticks — levers that move forward and backward and from side to side to control a machine.

loader — a vehicle that moves material using a wide bucket on the front.

mines — places where coal, gold, silver, and other things are taken out of the ground.

pistons — long metal tubes that slide inside larger tubes called cylinders. Engines and hydraulic arms use pistons.

radiators — devices that cool the liquid flowing through a engine, keeping the engine from getting too hot.

scraper — a vehicle that makes the ground level by scraping earth into a hopper and carrying it away.

screed — a large plate on a paving machine that smooths the concrete being laid down.

struts — long rods that provide support.

tracks — metal or rubber belts that circle around a row of wheels to move a machine.

transmission — the system in a vehicle that takes power from the engine and sends it to the wheels.

vibrates — shakes rapidly.

FOR MORE INFORMATION

Books

Bulldozers. Mighty Machines (series).
    Linda D. Williams (Pebble Plus)

Digger. Machines at Work (series).
    Nicola DesChamps (DK Publishing)

Dump Trucks. Pull Ahead Books (series).
    Judith Jango-Cohen (Lerner Publications)

Earth Movers. Mighty Movers (series).
    Sarah Tieck (Buddy Books)

Trucks, Tractors, and Cranes. How Science Works (series).
    Bryson Gore (Copper Beech Books)

Wheel Loaders. Earth Movers (series).
    Joanne Randolph (PowerKids Press)

Web Sites

JCB Junior
*www.jcb.com/(cl1xawa4tfneua55enouljmd)/jcbjunior/
    index.aspx*

Kikki's Workshop: Learn More About Construction
    Machines!
www.kenkenkikki.jp/e_index2.html

New York State Department of Transportation Kids Corner:
    Big Rigs
*www.dot.state.ny.us/reg/r6/i86_project/kids_site/
    bigrigs.html*

P&H Mining Equipment: P&H Photo Gallery
www.phmining.com/photos/index.html

INDEX